SIMPLE SCIENCE

Magnetism

Published by Creative Education
P.O. Box 227
Mankato, Minnesota 56002
Creative Education is an imprint of The Creative Company.

DESIGN AND PRODUCTION BY **ZENO DESIGN**

PHOTOGRAPHS BY Alamy (Garry Gary), Corbis, Getty Images (Binkley/
Kniza, Imagno/Contibutor, Werner Dieterich, Mitchell Funk, Peter Ginter,
Charles Gullung, Meyer Pfundt, Yamada Taro), Photo Researchers (Library
of Congress, David Parker, Science Source, Science Photo Library), Photri-
Microstock, Rainbow Photography (Coco McCoy), Stock Photos (Richard
Gilbert, Tom McCarthy), Tom Stack & Associates (NCAR/TSADO), Richard Goff,
Tom Myers, Bonnie Sue, D. Jeanene Tiner, Unicorn

LIBRARY OF CONGRESS CATALOGING-IN-PUBLICATION DATA

Frisch-Schmoll, Joy.
Magnetism / by Joy Frisch-Schmoll.
p. cm. — (Simple science)
Includes index.
ISBN 978-1-58341-577-1
1. Magnetism—Juvenile literature. I. Title. II. Series.

QC753.7.F75 2008
538—dc22   2007004185

First edition

9 8 7 6 5 4 3 2 1

SCIENCE

Magnetism

Joy Frisch-Schmoll

SIMPLE

CREATIVE C EDUCATION

Magnets (*MAG-nits*) are things that attract metal. "Attract" is a word that means "pulls on." People use magnets every day. A magnet attracts things made of a metal called **iron**.

Iron is used to make many things. Train tracks and hammers are made of iron. Frying pans are made of iron, too.

this rock is a kind of magnet

magnetism

Magnets are used in lots of places. Some magnets are easy to see. Other magnets are hidden inside things we use. Magnets are used in homes. They are used in schools, too.

THIS COMPUTER PART USES MAGNETS

MAGNETISM

People use magnets on refrigerator doors to hold notes in place. Refrigerator doors have long, skinny magnets, too. They make sure the doors stay shut tight.

Some metal things can be recycled, or used again. Magnets can pull metal objects like cans out of garbage.

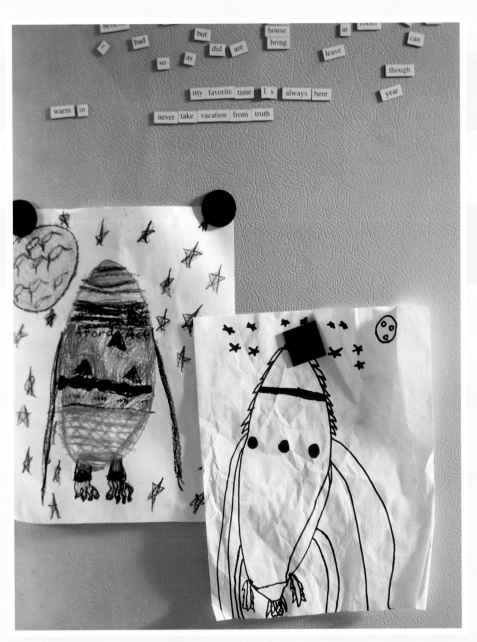

REFRIGERATORS CAN HOLD MAGNETS

Thales (*THAY-leez*) was a **scientist**

(*SI-en-tist*) who lived a long time ago. He

used magnets to pick up metal things.

The first **compass** (*KUM-pes*) was made

using magnets. A compass tells people

which direction is north.

Christopher Columbus was an explorer. He used a compass when he sailed his ship. Captains on ships still use compasses today.

A COMPASS SHOWS DIRECTIONS

MAGNETISM

Lots of machines are made with

electromagnets (*eh-lek-tro-MAG-nits*).

Electromagnets are magnets that can

be turned off and on. Cranes are tall

machines that use electromagnets. They

lift heavy things made of metal.

CRANES LIFT BIG ELECTROMAGNETS

MAGNETISM

Electricity (*eh-lek-TRIS-ih-tee*) is made using magnets. Special machines make magnets move fast close to iron. This makes electricity. Electricity is used in all kinds of buildings.

Dropping a magnet can hurt it. A dropped magnet can become weaker. It cannot attract iron as well.

ELECTRICITY LIGHTS UP BUILDINGS

MAGNETISM

A long time ago, there were no telephones. People used machines called telegraphs (*TEL-uh-grafs*) to send messages. An electromagnet moved a pen up and down. The pen drew dots and dashes on paper. The dots and dashes stood for letters that spelled a message.

TELEGRAPHS SENT OUT MESSAGES

MAGNETISM

Some magnets push things instead of pulling them. Scientists are trying to make special cars that float above roads with magnets. Trains that float above magnets have already been built. Electromagnets push the trains above a track and then pull them forward.

MAGNETS MAKE THIS TRAIN MOVE

MAGNETISM

Magnets are used in many ways today. They might be used in more ways in the future. Scientists know a lot about magnets. But they still have more to learn. Someday magnets might make life easier and more fun!

LOTS OF MACHINES USE MAGNETS

MAGNETISM

You can see which things are pulled by a magnet. Get a small magnet. Use it to try to pick up a nail, coin, and paper clip. Try to pick up a toothpick, glass marble, and metal spoon, too. The magnet will pick up the nail, paper clip, and spoon. It will not pick up the coin, toothpick, or marble. These things do not have iron in them.

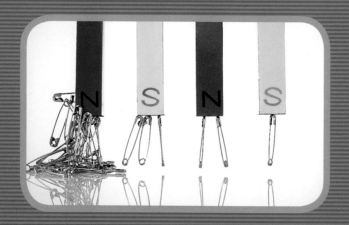

compass a tool that shows direction; it always points to the north

electricity a kind of power that makes lights and machines work

electromagnets strong magnets made with wire wrapped around iron

iron a strong metal that is used to make many things

scientist a person who learns about science

23

24

Columbus, Christopher **10**

compasses **10, 23**

cranes **12**

electricity **14, 23**

electromagnets **12, 16, 18, 23**

iron **4, 14, 22, 23**

metal **4, 8, 12**

refrigerators **8**

scientists **10, 18, 20, 23**

telegraphs **16**

Thales **10**

trains **18**